Flourishing in ....

To Cerys,

Praying for you as you journey
through the wilderness – God is
faithful !

Love

Alice

Flourishing in the Wilderness

Alice Swain

The Salvation Army
UNITED KINGDOM TERRITORY
WITH THE REPUBLIC OF IRELAND
101 Newington Causeway, London, SE1 6BN

Flourishing in the Wilderness
Alice Swain

First published in 2019 by
Shield Books
© The Salvation Army
United Kingdom Territory with the Republic of Ireland
101 Newington Causeway, London SE1 6BN

ISBN: 978-1-912981-01-4
Ebook ISBN: 978-1-912981-02-1

Book Editor: Rebecca Goldsmith
Cover Design: Mark Knight
Cover Image © Jordan Whitt on Unsplash

Registered charity no. 214779, and in Scotland SC009359

SHIELD
BOOKS
© The Salvation Army
United Kingdom Territory with
the Republic of Ireland

Printed and bound by
4bind Limited

Contents

Abbreviation of Bible Translations

NLT	New Living Translation
HCSB	Holman Christian Standard Bible
MSG	The Message
AMP	The Amplifed Bible
TPT	The Passion Translation
VOICE	The Voice

Introduction

THE title of this book has been birthed out of my own five-year journey through infertility and childlessness. Through this time I have experienced every one of the feelings, situations and emotions talked about in this book, and many more besides. However, God has been gently and graciously leading me to the understanding that through him we can all flourish in the wilderness. For each of us, our wilderness may look very different; it may be grief, divorce, illness, singleness or unemployment, to name but a few. However, the universal truth of God's word is true for each of us today.

God really started speaking into my heart about the idea of flourishing through my wilderness of infertility while I was on a pilgrimage to Israel in May 2017. As I sailed on the Sea of Galilee listening to a beautiful worship song, 'It is well', God reminded me that he who calmed the storm on those very waters still had the power to calm the storm that was raging in my life. Then days later, at the pools of Bethesda, while looking at a lone poppy growing in the rubble, I felt a sense of God's miraculous healing in my heart and I began to really see what flourishing in the wilderness may look like in my life.

In the summer of 2017, God started to speak to me about writing a book. It was a prospect that both daunted and excited me. However, as a woman in full-time ministry in The Salvation Army, running a busy centre and a growing church, I failed to see where I would ever find the time to write what God has placed on my heart. As God continued to place seeds of encouragement and ideas in my heart, I continued to tell him I simply didn't have the time to sit and commit to paper what I felt he was calling me to write. Then on a sunny August bank holiday Monday, as my husband and I (and of course my two fur babies) were leaving a quaint hotel in the country to discover the local area, I fell down a small step and managed to break my ankle very badly. Later that night as I lay in hospital after a five-and-a-half-hour-long operation with enough metal in my leg to make a transformer somewhat jealous, God spoke to me and said, 'I didn't cause this to happen, but … now you have plenty of time to write a book!' Through the six long months it took to recover, this book emerged. At times when I have felt unqualified, God has reminded me that 'I can do all things through Christ who strengthens me' (Philippians 4:13, *New King James Version*). At times when I have felt weak, God has reminded me: 'My grace is sufficient for you, for my power is made perfect in weakness' (2 Corinthians 12:9), and when I have felt far too small for such a large task he has shown me biblical characters such as David, Esther, Hannah, Noah, Moses and many more who did big things for God even though they felt small.

As I have written this book, God has placed a dream in my heart of men and women in the Church, and in particular The Salvation Army, coming together, sharing their stories and finding support as they navigate the difficulties of the wilderness in their own lives. I pray that we would see groups of people supporting and encouraging others to flourish, that we might weep with those who weep but also rejoice with those who rejoice. I really pray that through The Salvation Army women and men going through the wilderness may find an oasis. I pray that church to them will be a place where they feel understood, accepted and valued and that any damage done by well-meaning churches in the past may be healed and restoration would be found. God has given me a big heart and a big mouth 'for such a time as this', and I can't wait to hear from you as you delve into his word and study how you can flourish and bear fruit in your wilderness.

This book can be read on your own but it is even better if read with big cups of tea, large slices of cake and other people to share with. Each chapter ends with a song found in *The Song Book of the Salvation Army* and as I looked for each song I really found that they came alive and spoke, often prophetically, into each chapter.

I pray that the words so eloquently written by others may speak prophetically into your lives and give you a deeper understanding on your journey.

1

Flourishing in the wilderness

Life will flourish wherever this water flows.
Ezekiel 47:9, *NLT*

THROUGHOUT the Bible there is a lot of imagery of the wilderness. In the Old Testament we see the people of Israel spending 40 years in the wilderness while waiting to enter the Promised Land. In the New Testament we see Jesus go into the wilderness where he is tempted by the devil.

In the Scriptures, the wilderness is not just used to picture the physical environment, but it is often a metaphor for our spiritual and emotional health. The 40 years that the people of Israel spent in the desert was a time of discipline, where they were broken to understand submission to God, and they were encouraged to rely on God and not on themselves. For Jesus, his time in the wilderness was a time of great trial and suffering in preparation for his sacrifice ahead.

While on pilgrimage to Israel I was able to experience first-hand what the wilderness actually looks and feels like. It was hot, arid and desolate. There was simply mile after mile of nothing but barrenness. As I stood in the intense heat of the midday sun, I started to realise what it *really* meant to picture wilderness.

For us as Christians, we can sometimes feel as though we are stuck in the wilderness: bleak and desolate, with no hope for miles around.

Reading the book of Kings we see the prophet Elijah was not a stranger to being in the wilderness, spiritually as well as physically.

> Then he went on alone into the wilderness, travelling all day. He sat down under a solitary broom tree and prayed that he might die. 'I have had enough, Lord,' he said. 'Take my life, for I am no better than my ancestors who have already died.'
>
> 1 Kings 19:4, *NLT*

Elijah had done mighty things for God and had just had a real mountain-top experience. However, his wilderness mindset overtook him and he could see no goodness ahead. But throughout the chapter we see how God was there with him all along, even if he could not feel it. The angels brought him food and drink, and led him to a place of shelter. Then he had a beautiful experience of God, where God drew close to him in the still of the wilderness. He followed God's instructions, even though it meant returning to the wilderness, and God blessed him.

Alongside the barren imagery of the wilderness, we often see rich imagery of the wilderness giving way to a flourishing and fertile land. Very often the promise of God and his goodness is pictured as fruit growing in a barren land.

> Look, I am about to do something new; even now it is coming. Do you not see it? Indeed, I will make a way in the wilderness, rivers in the desert.
>
> Isaiah 43:19, *HCSB*

An encounter with God can cause a barren wilderness to become a flourishing place, where the water of life flows and ensures God's goodness is seen. When we allow the life-giving water of God to flow in our hearts, we can become physically and spiritually like the person in Psalm 1.

> Blessed is the one ... whose delight is in the law of the Lord, and who meditates on his law day and night. That person is like a tree planted by streams of water, which yields its fruits in season and whose leaf does not wither.
>
> Psalm 1:1–3

When we face difficult times in our lives, be it infertility, illness, divorce or whatever it might be, we can often feel our lives are arid and desolate; we seem to be utterly alone, as if we are in the wilderness.

There have been times in my own journey of infertility when I have felt as if I were stuck in the wilderness. Like the children of Israel, the journey I walked into motherhood, which I believed would only take a short while, seemed to go on for ever! At times I have felt abandoned by God and alone in my suffering. However, God wants to say to us today:

> The desert and the parched land will be glad; the wilderness will rejoice and blossom. Like the crocus, it will burst into bloom; it will rejoice greatly and shout for joy.
>
> Isaiah 35:1–2

We can all flourish in whatever wilderness we may face. What's more, God wants to help us to be fruitful, even if the landscape around us seems barren. The key to our flourishing is to draw close to God and spend time with him, in his word.

When we come to God and allow his living water to flow through the dry places, we can flourish and grow in him. Jeremiah 17 paints a beautiful picture. It is a picture that shows how we can flourish in the wilderness and have the strength to bear fruit even through the trials and difficulties that life can throw at us.

> But blessed is the man who trusts me, God, the woman who sticks with God. They're like trees replanted in Eden, putting down roots near the rivers – never a worry through the hottest of summers, never dropping a leaf, serene and calm through droughts, bearing fresh fruit every season.
>
> Jeremiah 17:7–8, *MSG*

Questions

1. Where in your life can you see a wilderness? How does it relate to wilderness imagery?

2. Read 1 Kings 19. How can you relate to this?

3. How can you flourish in your wilderness? What strategies can you use?

4. How does the following song relate to what we have thought about?

When shall I come unto the healing waters?
Lifting my heart, I cry to thee my prayer.
Spirit of peace, my Comforter and healer,
In whom my springs are found, let my soul meet thee there.

Chorus
From a hill I know,
Healing waters flow;
O rise, Immanuel's tide,
And my soul overflow!

Wash from my hands the dust of earthly striving;
Take from my mind the stress of secret fear;
Cleanse thou the wounds from all but thee far hidden,
And when the waters flow let my healing appear.

Light, life and love are in that healing fountain,
All I require to cleanse me and restore;
Flow through my soul, redeem its desert places,
And make a garden there for the Lord I adore.

Albert Orsborn
SASB 742

2

No idols

Jesus replied, 'Love the Lord your God with all your heart and with all your soul and with all your mind.'
Matthew 22:37

FROM the very beginning of God's relationship with his people, he made it clear that he wants to be the most important thing in our lives. When he created the Ten Commandments his first two rules were about him being the first priority in our lives.

> 'You shall have no other gods before me. You shall not make for yourself an image in the form of anything in heaven above or on the earth beneath or in the waters below. You shall not bow down to them or worship them; for I, the Lord your God, am a jealous God.'
> Exodus 20:3–5

God is jealous and doesn't want anything to get in the way of your relationship with him. In the Old Testament, God made it very clear to his people what an idol was – the above reading shows that it was any image or object that is worshipped instead of God. Throughout the Old Testament, we see God's people turning from him and worshipping idols before then realising the error of their ways.

In the New Testament we see idolatry is far more than just handmade 'gods'; it is to do with what it is we covet. The 'idols' we have may not be bad things in themselves, but when we desire them more than God, they become idols in our lives.

So put to death and deprive of power the evil longings of your earthly body [with its sensual, self-centred instincts] immorality, impurity, sinful passion, evil desire, and greed, which is [a kind of] idolatry [because it replaces your devotion to God].

Colossians 3:5, *AMP*

In Exodus 32 we see an interesting lesson about idolatry. As Moses ascended the mountain to receive the Ten Commandments, the Israelites, under Aaron's leadership, very quickly turned to idolatry. They melted down all of their jewellery and made an idol that they could worship. Their behaviour and attitude crumbled, and it caused God to become angry. Moses too was so angry that he broke the stone tablets with the commandments written on them.

The Israelites, when they made the golden calf, had not heard from God in a while. Moses their leader had been gone for some time, and this caused them to look to something else to take God's place. They assumed that their way was better than God's way, and so went their own way and put an idol in his place.

For many of us this can resonate with our own hearts. Sometimes we seem to receive few answers from God, or he seems silent. This can lead to us making our own plans and creating our own idols. Sometimes we just don't believe God is enough.

In the New Testament we see another example of a person struggling with idols. When the rich man came to Jesus in Mark 10:17–27, he wanted to know what he could do in order to live in the fullness of God's promise. Jesus made it clear that the key to eternal life is to put God before the things you love the most. Although he was a good man and was earnestly seeking God, he had a huge idol in his life – his money.

We can all fall easily into putting other things before God and making them something that we worship. The desire we may have for a husband, child, house, health or wealth may be a healthy one; however, if it takes God's place and becomes an idol, then we go against God's word.

We need to be careful to ensure that we do not let other things get in the way of our love for God. We are warned in 1 John 5:21: 'Little children (believers, dear ones), guard yourselves from idols – [false teachings, moral compromises, and anything that would take God's place in your heart]' (*AMP*).

We must meditate on God's word and fix our eyes on him, for he loves us and desires only good things for us. We must cling to God and be part of him like branches on a vine.

'I am the vine; you are the branches. If you remain in me and I in you, you will bear much fruit; apart from me you can do nothing.'
John 15:5

Questions

1. What things in our own life can become idols?
2. Can you relate to the Israelites or the rich man who met Jesus in any way?
3. What strategies can you put in place to ensure things do not get in the way of your love for God?
4. How does the following song relate to what we have thought about?

O Jesus, I have promised
To serve thee to the end,
Be thou for ever near me,
My Master and my friend.
I shall not fear the battle
If thou art by my side,
Nor wander from the pathway
If thou wilt be my guide.

O let me feel thee near me;
The world is ever near;
I see the sights that dazzle,
The tempting sounds I hear.
My foes are ever near me,
Around me and within;
But, Jesus, draw thou nearer
And shield my soul from sin.

O let me hear thee speaking
In accents clear and still,
Above the storms of passion,
The murmurs of self-will.
O speak to reassure me,
To chasten or control;
O speak to make me listen,
Thou Guardian of my soul.

O Jesus, thou hast promised
To all who follow thee,
That where thou art in Glory
There shall thy servant be;
And, Jesus, I have promised
To serve thee to the end;
O give me grace to follow,
My Master and my friend.

John Ernest Bode
SASB 613

3

Jealousy

A tranquil heart is life to the body, but jealousy is rottenness to the bones.

Proverbs 14:30, *HCSB*

AS we are going through life, and navigating the wilderness, it can be so difficult to fight the feelings of jealousy when other people seem to achieve easily the things we desire. For me, navigating the wilderness of infertility, when I see a bump on a mum-to-be, I can so easily feel a twinge of jealousy and envy as I wish it were me.

Scripture tells us the stories of people who battled with jealousy and the effect it had on their lives. Two examples we will look at both revolve around women who were struggling to conceive and who let their jealousy give way to bitterness.

In Genesis 16 we see how jealousy and bitterness grew between Sarai and Hagar. Sarai had been promised a son by God but she had grown tired of waiting. She took matters into her own hands and encouraged her husband to sleep with Hagar, their servant. Hagar became pregnant and the relationship between the two ladies became bitter – it 'rotted their bones'.

> When Hagar knew she was pregnant, she began to treat her mistress, Sarai, with contempt.
>
> Genesis 16:4, *NLT*

Due to Hagar's feelings towards Sarai, later called Sarah, Sarai retreated and took action.

> Then Sarai treated Hagar so harshly that she finally ran away.
>
> Genesis 16:6, *NLT*

The jealousy and bitterness between the two women festered for years and it affected the people around them. Sarah's jealousy of Ishmael, Hagar's son, grew so much that even in times of celebration, when God had given her the son she was promised, she could not get over her feelings. Sarah struggled so much that in the end, Hagar and Ishmael were sent away.

Later in the book of Genesis, we meet two other women who battled with their feelings of envy and bitterness. Rachel and Leah were sisters. A man called Jacob fell in love with Rachel, but due to deception, he married Leah. This began great jealousy between the two of them.

Rachel later married Jacob, which made Leah jealous as he loved Rachel more. Leah believed that by her having children he would love her more than Rachel.

> So Leah became pregnant and gave birth to a son. She named him Reuben, for she said, 'The Lord has noticed my misery, and now my husband will love me.'
>
> Genesis 29:32, *NLT*

This made Rachel even more bitter and envious as she struggled to conceive. Every pregnancy of Leah and every birth made Rachel's jealousy increase. She was full of sorrow for her failure to bear a child, while everyone around her was fruitful. It became too much to bear.

> When Rachel saw that she wasn't having any children for Jacob, she became jealous of her sister. She pleaded with Jacob, 'Give me children, or I'll die!'
>
> Genesis 30:1, *NLT*

Rachel's sorrow led to a deep jealousy and bitterness, and although she did eventually conceive, the jealousy between the two women made for a very unhappy family that affected generations to come.

We see from the word of God that jealousy towards others is not good for us.

> For where you have envy and selfish ambition, there you find disorder and every evil practice.
>
> James 3:16

Jealousy is not something that comes from God and, as we have seen in the life of the women we have looked at, it has the potential to cause hurt, pain and broken relationships. As our first Scripture says, it rots the bones!

Often our jealousy has more to do with ourselves than the other person. When we highlight the things that others have, it is because of the void we feel in our own life. Often when we feel jealousy – when we see that pregnancy announcement, or that picture of the 'perfect family', or when we see that person being promoted in work or moving into that brand new house – it isn't because the person is not nice, it's because we just sincerely wish that person was us.

In those times when bitterness creeps in, we must remember that God is a good God. He will not forsake us; we need to cry out to him.

> Let the dawning day bring me revelation of your tender, *unfailing love*.
>
> Psalm 143:8, *TPT*

The answer to combating jealousy is love! When we see the picture of what love is in 1 Corinthians 13, we see that love is not jealous. We must practise loving God, but also loving those people we are jealous of.

> Above all, love each other deeply, because love covers over a multitude of sins.
>
> 1 Peter 4:8

That may sound impossible, and it really is tough, but for ourselves and the people around us, we must commit to loving others and make jealousy flee. Does it feel hard?

But he said to me, 'My grace is sufficient for you, for my power is made perfect in weakness'.

2 Corinthians 12:9

Questions

1. In what areas have you struggled or do you struggle with jealousy?
2. Do you relate to either of our biblical examples? How?
3. How can we practise love to overcome jealousy?
4. How does the following song relate to what we have thought about?

At the moment of my weakness,
When my need for power is plain,
And my own strength is exhausted once again,
Then my Lord has made provision for the day of my despair,
And his precious Holy Spirit hears my prayer.

Chorus
Holy Spirit! Promised presence fall on me.
Holy Spirit! Make me all I long to be.
Holy Spirit! Holy Spirit!
Give your power to me, O Holy Spirit.

When the darkness falls around me,
When bewildered and afraid,
When I feel the most deserted and betrayed,
Then my every need is answered by God's providential care,
And his precious Holy Spirit hears my prayer.

Nothing now can rob God's servant
Of the peace that he bequeaths,
Nothing take away the strength his presence breathes.
Of the everlasting arms of love I'm daily made aware,
And his precious Holy Spirit hears my prayer.

John Gowans
SASB 316

4

Alone

How long, Lord? Will you forget me for ever?
How long will you hide your face from me?
How long must I wrestle with my thoughts
And day after day have sorrow in my heart?
How long will my enemy triumph over me?
Psalm 13:1–2

HAVE you ever been in a crowded room and yet felt completely alone? Have there been times in your life where you have struggled with loneliness and feelings of unworthiness? Most of us would admit that we have had times when Psalm 13 seems to resonate with our heart.

Often our time in the wilderness is a very lonely one. I have found in my own journey through infertility that I seem to be excluded from the 'club of motherhood', and often the shame and intimacy of the issues I face means I often feel completely alone. We can all feel forgotten.

Throughout the Scriptures we see people battling with loneliness. Jeremiah the prophet often felt lonely and depressed. He received hard and costly instructions from God on how to live his life. He was told he must not marry or have children while he was sharing God's word. Many of his friends turned against him and he was well and truly alone. The following verses are some that we can relate to when we are struggling with loneliness.

I never sat in the company of revellers, never made merry with them; I sat alone because your hand was on me and you had filled me with indignation. Why is my pain unending and my wound grievous and incurable? You are to me like a deceptive brook, like a spring that fails.

Jeremiah 15:17–18

Jeremiah didn't have it easy and he struggled. He was not quiet in sharing with God his struggles and feelings of loneliness. However, he often came back to the understanding that God was using him and is a powerful, almighty God. Even though, by earthly standards, Jeremiah was completely alone, he understood God was with him. This is often echoed in Scripture.

But look at this: you are still holding my right hand;
you have been all along.
Even though I was angry and hard-hearted, you gave me good advice;
when it's all over, you will receive me into your glory.
For all my wanting, I don't have anyone but you in heaven.
There is nothing on earth that I desire other than you.
I admit how broken I am in body and spirit,
but God is my strength, and he will be mine forever …
But the closer I am to you, my God, the better because life with you is good.
O Lord, the Eternal, you keep me safe –
I will tell everyone what you have done.

Psalm 73:23–26, 28, *VOICE*

When Jesus came to Earth as a man, he also had times of loneliness. Many people in society didn't understand him; in fact they despised him. His disciples, his closest friends, often didn't 'get it' and he was so often misunderstood. When he was hanging on the cross, dying, he felt well and truly alone, as if even his Father had abandoned him. At that moment he cried: 'My God, my God, why have you forsaken me?' (Matthew 27:46). He understood a loneliness beyond anything we can comprehend.

When we feel as if we are in a pit of loneliness, we can remember that Jesus completely understands. He has felt exactly as we feel.

One of the other wonderful things about Jesus is that when he came to Earth, he came as Emmanuel – meaning God with us. He came, died and rose again so that we would never be alone. When he commissioned his disciples, he made it clear when he said: 'Surely I am with you always, to the very end of the age' (Matthew 28:20).In the days when we feel alone, and at the very moment we feel incredibly isolated and forgotten, we must remember that God is always with us. We are never alone.

> Where can I go from your Spirit?
> Where can I flee from your presence?
> If I go up to the heavens, you are there;
> if I make my bed in the depths, you are there.
> If I rise on the wings of the dawn,
> if I settle on the far side of the sea,
> even there your hand will guide me,
> your right hand will hold me fast.
> If I say, 'Surely the darkness will hide me
> and the light become night around me,'
> even the darkness will not be dark to you;
> the night will shine like the day,
> for darkness is as light to you.
>
> Psalm 139:7–12

Questions

1. Can you name other Bible characters who suffered with loneliness? What was their story?

2. How has Jesus given you comfort in loneliness? Can you share any Scripture verses?

3. How can you reach out to others when you feel lonely? Take time to pray for people in your life who may be feeling lonely.

4. How does the following song relate to what we have thought about?

Do you sometimes feel that no one truly knows you,
And that no one understands or really cares?
Through his people, God himself is close beside you,
And through them he plans to answer all your prayers.

Chorus
Someone cares, someone cares,
Someone knows your deepest need, your burden shares;
Someone cares, someone cares,
God himself will hear the whisper of your prayers.

Ours is not a distant God, remote, unfeeling,
Who is careless of our loneliness and pain,
Through the ministry of men he gives his healing,
In their dedicated hands brings hope again.

John Gowans
SASB 10

5

If only

'Seek first his kingdom and his righteousness, and all these things will be given to you as well.'

Matthew 6:33

SOMETIMES in our Christian journey we can fall into the trap of thinking, 'if only … happens, I will be complete and full.' For some, that 'thing' may be a baby, which in itself is a beautiful thing to hope for. However, it could be a happier marriage, a new ministry or job opportunity or one of many other things.

Some days our 'if only' seems to overtake our minds. We become so determined to reach our goal that it is the only thing we are able to think about. Sometimes our 'if only' becomes our main focus and we lose sight of God because we are concentrating on fulfilling our own goal.

There are times when our mind can easily become clouded by the things we desire, and we can start to believe that only when we get what we wish will we truly become complete. The Bible, however, makes it clear that completeness comes through Christ Jesus alone. Our families, ministries and goals are a great blessing, but they alone won't make us complete.

> So you also are complete through your union with Christ, who is the head over every ruler and authority.
>
> Colossians 2:10, *NLT*

It is only through Jesus and seeking him first that we can be complete. He is our source for all the things we need. When we look to the life of Jesus, we see that he made it his business to make people complete. Time and time again through the Gospels we see that when people came to him, not only did he heal them physically, but he also healed them emotionally and spiritually. He made each of them whole. Very often people came to him with a physical problem but he could see the 'if only' in their hearts. God wants us to be complete in him, and that has been seen throughout the Scriptures.

> I will give them an undivided heart and put a new spirit in them; I will remove from them their heart of stone and give them a heart of flesh.
>
> Ezekiel 11:19

Sometimes, even though God promises us an undivided heart, complete in him, we can try to take our 'if only' into our own hands. We are certainly not the first people to do this. Sarah, in the Old Testament, was guilty of thinking on the 'if only' and doubting God's promises. She knew God had promised her and her husband a son, but she became so single-minded about her 'if only' that she encouraged her husband to have a child with her servant. This had huge consequences for her and her family. The desire for a son was not a bad thing at all but, when she failed to put God's Kingdom first, she diverted from his path for her life.

Thankfully, we serve a mighty God who wants to make us complete, even when we mess up and put our 'if only' before him. God's desire for us to be complete was so strong that he sent his Son to become flesh and dwell among us.

Jesus knows our 'if onlys' and how we sometimes battle to keep them from our mind. When Jesus was in the garden of Gethsemane, he prayed saying:

> 'My Father, *if* it is possible, may this cup be taken from me. Yet not as I will, but as you will.'
>
> Matthew 26:39

Jesus understands that life isn't always easy, but our Bible reading promises that when we seek his Kingdom first, all our 'if onlys' will be looked after by him. It may not always seem easy, but God's word is true.

We all have our own 'if only'; be it the hope for a child, a better marriage, more fulfilling work. They are all great things, but we must always seek God and his completeness in our lives. God is trying to teach us something new every single day. Do not miss out on completeness in him by thinking 'if only'!

Today this is my prayer for you:

> And I pray that you, being rooted and established in love, may have power, together with all the Lord's holy people, to grasp how wide and long and high and deep is the love of Christ, and to know this love that surpasses knowledge – that you may be *filled to the measure of all the fullness of God.*
>
> Ephesians 3:17–19

Questions

1. What 'if only' threatens to take over your heart?
2. Which of the healings of Jesus speak to you about completeness in Christ?
3. What strategies can you use to seek God's Kingdom first?
4. How does the following song relate to what we have thought about?

> *All I once held dear, built my life upon,*
> *All this world reveres, and wars to own,*
> *All I once thought gain I have counted loss;*
> *Spent and worthless now, compared to this:*

Chorus
Knowing you, Jesus, knowing you,
There is no greater thing.
You're my all, you're the best,
You're my joy, my righteousness,
And I love you, Lord.

Now my heart's desire is to know you more,
To be found in you and known as yours,
To possess by faith what I could not earn,
All-surpassing gift of righteousness.

O, to know the power of your risen life,
And to know you in your sufferings,
To become like you in your death, my Lord,
So with you to live and never die.

Graham Kendrick
SASB 565

6

Love is all you need

There is no fear in love. But perfect love drives out fear.
1 John 4:18–19

WE live in a world full of fear. We only have to watch the news to see that many people live in fear. Living in a society bursting with fear, we can all become fearful. Fearful that we don't meet society's expectations, fearful that we aren't 'good enough' and fearful that we may never have the things we truly desire.

Fear is a topic often spoken about in the pages of the Bible, and time and time again we are told to 'fear not'. However, we can often feel confused. How can we 'fear not' in a world where we are surrounded by fear both inside and out?

The answer comes in complete simplicity – 'Perfect love drives out fear.'

As a woman married to a man from Liverpool, it is expected I should have a love for the band The Beatles, and I do! One of their most famous songs stated 'All you need is love', and this is true for us as people in Christ; all we need is the perfect love of God. Looking to the Bible, we see some beautiful pictures of what this love is like.

Love is large and incredibly patient. Love is gentle and consistently kind to all. It refuses to be jealous when blessing comes to someone else. Love does not brag about one's achievements nor inflate its own importance. Love does not traffic in shame and disrespect, nor selfishly seek its own honour. Love is not easily irritated or quick to take offence. Love joyfully celebrates honesty and finds no delight in what is wrong. Love is a safe place of shelter, for it never stops believing the best for others. Love never takes failure as defeat, for it never gives up. Love never stops loving.

1 Corinthians 13:4–8, *TPT*

This is a stunning picture of the cure for fear. It is trusting in the perfect love that we have just read about. The truly amazing thing about this love is that the Bible also says: 'Whoever does not love does not know God, because *God is love*' (1 John 4:8).

If perfect love casts out all fear and God is love, then we can see that God can help us to live a life free from fear. When we allow God's love to consume us, when our desire is to love God and his word and follow his ways, then fear will not stand a chance!

Only God has a perfect love. We cannot find it in friendships, relationships, objects, or even that thing that we desire. Often in life we look to earthly things to drive out our fear from our heart and mind. We rely on people around us, but this can leave us feeling more afraid and hurt as they let us down (and, as imperfect people, they inevitably will).

However, God in his word tells us that he will never let us down and will be with us in *all* circumstances – even the ones we fear the most.

> Even in the *unending* shadows of death's darkness,
>   I am not overcome by fear.
> Because you are with me *in those dark moments*,
>   near with your protection and guidance,
>   I am comforted.
>
> Psalm 23:4, *VOICE*

God's love can take away our fear in any situation. But it doesn't end there! When we love others, striving to show God's perfect love, we will see fear disappear in those situations. Do you fear loneliness? Love everyone you meet, asking for God's perfect love. Do you fear being childless? Love those around you, both mothers and those waiting to be mothers, and show God's great love. Do you fear that you are not good enough? Love those around you as if they are God's favourite and you will realise that you are good enough … more than that, you are his favourite!

When we focus on loving God and others, we will watch the fears float away and can rest in his love, filled with hope.

> Yes, my soul, find rest in God;
> my hope comes from him.
> Truly he is my rock and my salvation;
> he is my fortress, I shall not be shaken.
> My salvation and my honour depend on God;
> he is my mighty rock, my refuge.
> Trust in him at all times, you people;
> pour out your hearts to him,
> for God is our refuge.
>
> Psalm 62:5–8

Questions

1. What things do you fear in your everyday life?
2. Look again at 1 Corinthians 13. Replace 'Love is' with 'God is'. How does this change the way you view God and his love for you?
3. In which fearful situations can you show God's perfect love?
4. How does the following song relate to what we have thought about?

> *God's love to me is wonderful,*
> *That he should deign to hear*
> *The faintest whisper of my heart,*
> *Wipe from mine eyes the tear;*

And though I cannot comprehend
Such love, so great, so deep,
In his strong hands my soul I trust,
He will not fail to keep.

Chorus
God's love is wonderful,
God's love is wonderful,
Wonderful that he should give his Son to die for me;
God's love is wonderful!

God's love to me is wonderful!
My very steps are planned;
When mists of doubt encompass me,
I hold my Father's hand.
His love has banished every fear,
In freedom I rejoice,
And with my quickened ears I hear
The music of his voice.

God's love to me is wonderful!
He lights the darkest way;
I now enjoy his fellowship,
'Twill last through endless day.
My father doth not ask that I
Great gifts on him bestow,
But only that I love him too,
And serve him here below.

Sidney Edward Cox
SASB 25

7

Thinking right

Finally, brothers and sisters, whatever is true, whatever is noble, whatever is right, whatever is pure, whatever is lovely, whatever is admirable – if anything is excellent or praiseworthy – think about such things.

Philippians 4:8

HAVE you ever thought about what you think about? If you counted up the topics of the things you dwell on, what would your top ones be? Worries? Fear? Sorrow? We are all guilty of spending far too much time worrying and often our minds can be full of negative thoughts.

Our thoughts directly affect the things we say and do. If we are constantly bound up with worry, fear and sorrow, things can become so negative. In this verse we are told what we should be thinking about. If we begin to focus on things that are true, noble, right, pure, lovely, admirable, excellent and praiseworthy, we will start to look at and react to life in a different way.

We are in a battle and it is taking place in our mind. The devil wants us to think negatively and will try and tell us lies in order to encourage us to think on things which will bring sorrow, fear and a mind full of negativity.

From the beginning of God's word, we clearly see how the devil tried to encourage humanity to think negatively and act upon it. When Eve met the serpent in the garden of Eden, it immediately made her question God's love for her and the instructions she had been given.

> When the woman saw that the fruit of the tree was good for food and pleasing to the eye, and also desirable for growing wisdom, she took some and ate it. She also gave some to her husband, who was with her, and he ate it.
>
> Genesis 3:6

This began a pattern for us where the devil tries to take advantage of our mind by telling us lies. The sad thing is we so often believe them. For many of us, it seems easier to believe the lies of the enemy rather than the truth of the Saviour.

Jesus, in his time on Earth, also faced the lies of the enemy when he was tempted in the desert. However, every time the devil tried to get him to question his father, he responded, 'It is written'. The key for Jesus, and the key for each of us today, is to think upon the true, noble, right, pure, lovely, admirable, excellent and praiseworthy things that we read in the word of God.

The true word of God is a gift that can bring life to us and the situations we face:

> He chose to give birth to us by giving us his true word. And we, out of all creation, became his prized possession.
>
> James 1:18, *NLT*

You are a masterpiece! You are a prized possession of God. We need to replace each of the lies of the enemy with the truth of Christ. We need to fight the battle in our mind, and God calls us to never give up. Some days you may feel like you are losing but never forget, Christ has already won the war!

> We demolish arguments and every pretension that sets itself up against the knowledge of God, and we take captive every thought to make it obedient to Christ.
>
> 2 Corinthians 10:5

By thinking on the word of God and all of the things God tells us to think about, we are able to take captive every thought that is contrary. We take hold of that power to demolish the lies of the enemy and change our attitude, even in the difficult times.

We serve a gracious God who is always giving us what we need to succeed. When we begin to take our thoughts captive we may feel like we are failing miserably but we are always changing from glory to glory, and we are being transformed as our mind is constantly renewed.

> Do not conform to the pattern of this world, but be transformed by the renewing of your mind.
>
> Romans 12:2

So, today, when you start to have negative thoughts, try to replace them with thoughts that are positive. Better still, take them captive with the word of God.

Questions

1. Spend some time thinking about what is often on your mind. What are the top three things on your list?
2. What are the true, noble, right, pure, lovely, admirable, excellent and praiseworthy things that you can think about in difficult times?
3. What Bible verses help you to take every negative thought captive?
4. How does the following song relate to what we have thought about?

Lord, I come to you,
Let my heart be changed, renewed,
Flowing from the grace that I found in you.
And Lord, I've come to know
The weaknesses I see in me
Will be stripped away by the power of your love.

Chorus
Hold me close,
Let your love surround me.
Bring me near, draw me to your side.
And as I wait, I'll rise up like the eagle,
And I will soar with you,
Your Spirit leads me on in the power of your love.

Lord, unveil my eyes,
Let me see you face to face,
The knowledge of your love as you live in me.
Lord, renew my mind
As your will unfolds in my life,
In living every day in the power of your love.

Geoff Bullock
SASB 601

8

Stand firm

**Finally, be strong in the Lord and in his mighty power.
Put on the full armour of God, so that you can take your
stand against the devil's schemes. For our struggle is not
against flesh and blood, but against the rulers, against the
authorities, against the powers of this dark world and against
the spiritual forces of evil in the heavenly realms. Therefore
put on the full armour of God, so that when the day of evil
comes, you may be able to stand your ground, and after you
have done everything, to stand. Stand firm then.**
Ephesians 6:10–14

HAVE you ever tried to stand still in the wind as it gusts around
you? Or have you tried to stand still in the sea as the waves crashed
around you? It can take all your strength to stay standing.

Have you ever felt buffeted by circumstances, in the gust of
struggle and weighed down by grief? Have you had one of those
days when getting out of bed seems too tough and all you can do
is pull the duvet over your head? I know that feeling well!

When times get tough and disaster strikes our lives, we may feel
as if the waves are buffeting around us and the wind is taking our
breath away. We believe in the promises of God and the truth in the
Bible but there are situations in our life that can feel well and truly
overwhelming. Sometimes it can feel impossible to stand. When
we see another negative pregnancy test; suffer the grief of loss; fail
to get that interview or struggle to succeed in our marriage, we
may feel like we will never be able to stand again.

The passage from Ephesians 6 shows us that we can be strong in the Lord and stand through difficult situations. The instruction to stand comes four times in this passage, so we can tell it is important. It is not through our own strength that we do this, but through the Lord and his power. God will give you the strength you need in order not only to stand but to stand firm.

We are not battling physical things, but we are fighting against the devil. When we face difficulties, the devil will try every scheme he can to bring us to our knees. But the word makes it clear: '... after you have done everything, to stand. Stand firm.'

One character who chose to stand, even if his life was a risk, was Daniel. He chose to worship God, despite the threat of death, and he fought against the devil's schemes. He was brave and, even when he was told he was unable to pray any more, he refused to hide.

> Now when Daniel learned that the decree had been published, he went home to his upstairs room where the windows opened towards Jerusalem. Three times a day he got down on his knees and prayed, giving thanks to his God, just as he had done before. Then these men went as a group and found Daniel praying and asking God for help.
> Daniel 6:10–11

As Daniel entered into battles for God, things seemed to get even worse. When he was thrown in the lions' den, I'm sure he felt like he was being blown by the wind and buffeted by the waves. However, he stood firm and God miraculously brought him through a seemingly impossible situation.

In order to stand firm we need to be equipped in the armour of God and use the weapons that he gives. Like Daniel, we need to get on our knees in prayer and ask for his help.

The key to standing firm is not doing it alone. God will always be with you and will fight your battles for you. He asks you to stand but will be there to help you in those times you feel that you can't do it on your own. We have a tendency to try and take things into our own hands and do things our own way, but the Bible is clear:

'The Lord will fight for you; you need only to be still.' (Exodus 14:14) – or, I would say, 'stand and be still.'

In those tough situations we find ourselves in, when the pressures of life are overwhelming, in those times when the winds seem to blow us around and we struggle to stand, we must remember that like Daniel in the lions' den, Jesus will be right next to us, fighting for us and holding us up. A favourite Christian author of mine put it in such a great way, and we should try and remember it in every battle:

> Stand firm in the Lord, stand firm and let him fight your battle. Do not try to fight alone.
>
> (Francine Rivers, *A Voice in the Wind*)

Questions

1. Have you ever had an experience of extreme wind and waves? How did you feel?
2. How can you relate to Daniel and the situation he faced?
3. Why can it be difficult to allow God to fight for you?
4. How does the following song relate to what we have thought about?

> *When you feel weakest, dangers surround,*
> *Subtle temptations, troubles abound,*
> *Nothing seems hopeful, nothing seems glad,*
> *All is despairing, everything sad:*
>
> *Chorus*
> Keep on believing, Jesus is near;
> Keep on believing, there's nothing to fear;
> Keep on believing, this is the way;
> Faith in the night as well as the day.

If all were easy, if all were bright,
Where would the cross be, and where the fight?
But in the hardness, God gives to you
Chances of proving that you are true.

God is your wisdom, God is your might,
God's ever near you, guiding aright;
He understands you, knows all you need;
Trusting in him you'll surely succeed.

Let us press on then, never despair,
Live above feeling, victory's there;
Jesus can keep us so near to him
That nevermore our faith shall grow dim.

Lucy Milward Booth-Hellberg
SASB 691

9

Rejoice

Rejoice in the Lord always. I will say it again: rejoice!
Philippians 4:4

THERE are times in our lives that are full of joy and we can't help but praise God for all he has done. When we are feeling particularly close to God, our joy becomes apparent in every aspect of our life.

However, it isn't always easy to rejoice in the Lord when we are suffering. When things are difficult and tragedy strikes, praising God and rejoicing in him can be the last thing on our mind. When in the depths of pain and grief, a heart that rejoices may seem impossible.

You are not alone! Through the Bible we see people who struggled, like us, to rejoice when things got tough. In Psalms we see some great examples of how people chose to rejoice even when they did not feel it.

> So then, my soul, why would you be depressed?
> Why would you sink into despair?
> Just keep hoping and waiting on God, your Saviour.
> For no matter what, I will still sing with praise,
> for living before his face is my saving grace!
>
> Psalm 42:5, *TPT*

When we rejoice in God through the storm, we find a peace and strength that only he can bring. God is bigger than all of our problems, and praising God helps us to remember this. It develops our character and helps us to deal with difficult times that will help bring glory to him in the future.

> Don't run from tests and hardships, brothers and sisters. As difficult as they are, you will ultimately find joy in them; if you embrace them, your faith will blossom under pressure and teach you true patience as you endure. And true patience brought on by endurance will equip you to complete the long journey and cross the finish line – mature, complete, and wanting nothing.
>
> James 1:2–4, *VOICE*

Rejoicing in the Lord always is a constant choice. Through the tough times we need to consciously choose to trust in him and praise his name. Sometimes we are called to choose joy regardless of the circumstance.

> Though the fig-tree does not bud
> and there are no grapes on the vines,
> though the olive crop fails
> and the fields produce no food,
> though there are no sheep in the sheepfold
> and no cattle in the stalls,
> yet I will rejoice in the Lord,
> I will be joyful in God my Saviour.
>
> Habakkuk 3:17–18

As we face difficult times, we must find things to rejoice in, even if they are little things. Sometimes it may feel like a costly 'sacrifice of praise', but as we start to have an attitude of gratitude our attention will shift. We must be thankful – it may be a nice hot cup of coffee or a beautiful sunset. Whatever it may be, we must take the opportunity to praise God for all the things he has given to us.

When we are facing difficulties, when the ache of childlessness is great, the pain of grief threatens to overwhelm or the stress of trying to do everything perfectly seems too great, it is so easy to believe that God has forgotten us. We can feel completely alone and misunderstood. Everyone around us has the things we desire, and we can feel unloved. However, when we live a lifestyle of praise and rejoicing, we realise this isn't the case.

> Friends, when life gets really difficult, don't jump to the conclusion that God isn't on the job. Instead, be glad that you are in the very thick of what Christ experienced. This is a spiritual refining process, with glory just around the corner.
>
> 1 Peter 4:12–13, *MSG*

When we cling to God through every circumstance we will see the glory of God in our lives.

Questions

1. Have you had times in your life when you have struggled to rejoice? Why was it so difficult?
2. What situations do you need to choose to rejoice in today?
3. Write a list of three things you are thankful for, no matter how small.
4. How does the following song relate to what we have thought about?

For the beauty of the earth,
For the beauty of the skies,
For the love which from our birth
Over and around us lies,
Father, unto thee we raise
This our sacrifice of praise.

For the beauty of each hour
Of the day and of the night,
Hill and vale and tree and flower,
Sun and moon and stars of light,
Father, unto thee we raise
This our sacrifice of praise.

For the joy of ear and eye,
For the heart and mind's delight,
For the mystic harmony
Linking sense to sound and sight,
Father, unto thee we raise
This our sacrifice of praise.

For the joy of human love,
Brother, sister, parent, child,
Friends on earth, and friends above,
For all gentle thoughts and mild,
Father, unto thee we raise
This our sacrifice of praise.

For each perfect gift of thine
To our race so freely given,
Graces human and divine,
Flowers of earth and buds of Heaven.
Father, unto thee we raise
This our sacrifice of praise.

Folliott Sandford Pierpoint
SASB 14

10

Words of life

Do everything without grumbling or arguing, so that you may become blameless and pure, 'children of God without fault in a warped and crooked generation.' Then you will shine among them like stars in the sky as you hold firmly to the word of life.'
Philippians 2:14–16

WHEN life is tough and things seem unfair, our life can slip into an attitude of moaning. Looking at others and moaning about how rough we have it can make us feel better, if only for a little while. Grumbling can seem so easy to do, and sometimes it is out of our mouth before we even think about it.

A negative mindset can present itself in our grumbling and moaning. Complaining can make us feel justified in our difficulties. Our negative emotions spill out into every aspect of our lives, and our friends and family often suffer. To the world, complaining can be seen as right, and is generally encouraged, but when we consider how it makes us feel and when we look to the word of God, we can see that moaning is not what God intended for us.

God calls us to live a lifestyle radically different from that which we see in the world today. This lifestyle calls us to replace words of grumbling and complaint with words of life. In order to do this we need to know God's word and hold it close to our hearts. From near the beginning of the Bible this has been clear.

Keep this Book of Law always on your lips; meditate on it day and night, so that you may be careful to do everything written in it.
Joshua 1:8

It is important that we spend time in God's word daily and use creative ways to help it come alive for us. Here are five ways we can hold on firmly to his word of life.

Read his word: The Bible is a library of 66 books. It has everything from poetry to action. But more than that, it is the living, breathing word of God. We must spend time deep in Scripture and cling to the life we find in its pages.

> For we have the living Word of God, which is full of energy, and it pierces more sharply than a two-edged sword. It will even penetrate to the very core of our being where soul and spirit, bone and marrow meet! It interprets and reveals the true thoughts and secret motives of our hearts.
>
> Hebrew 4:12, *TPT*

Listen to the word: There are so many great speakers out there and their teaching is widely available online. Their passion for the word will most certainly help to fan your flame for the Bible. Listen to them while ironing, driving or getting dressed! Immerse yourself and you will find your desire for his word will grow.

Write the word: I love to write. I write in journals, in letters, in blogs. I have found that by writing down the word of God, it comes alive to me. Start to write out the word of God. Put affirming Scriptures on your mirror, tape Scriptures of praise to the fridge. When you write out Scripture, not only will you see it and be more likely to remember it, but others will see it too. Keep a journal and write your favourite Scriptures. It is good to look back in time and see what God has done.

Study the word creatively: We need to commit to studying the word of God. It is important to find the background and context of the word. When we understand the culture and times of the word it can really come alive. If you love to study and find this easy, then great! If you don't, all is not lost! There are many creative ways to study the word of God. Using art to explore Scripture can be really fulfilling, or writing songs based on what is written. Even discussing the word over a cup of coffee can bring a new perspective. Don't compare yourself to others. Do what is right for you.

Speak the word: Our words have power.

> The tongue has the power of life and death, and those who love it will eat its fruit.
>
> Proverbs 18:21

When we speak out words of life, they will have power over our problems. Declaring the victory of God over every challenge we face will remind us of God's power and shift the spiritual atmosphere.

When we live a life that has Christ at the centre, as we become more like him and cling to his word, we start to stand out. We shine like stars in the darkness. We often spend a lot of our time in places of grief and shame and it can be a privilege to be the light in those places. So take courage in his word.

> We are hard pressed on every side, but not crushed; perplexed, but not in despair; persecuted, but not abandoned; struck down, but not destroyed.
>
> 2 Corinthians 4:8–9

Questions

1. How can we stop ourselves from grumbling and complaining?
2. Do you ever struggle to keep the word of the Lord alive in your life? How do you combat this?
3. In what areas of your life do you need to shine like stars?

4. How does the following song relate to what we have thought about?

> Lord, thy word abideth,
> And our footsteps guideth;
> Who its truth believeth
> Light and joy receiveth.
>
> When our foes are near us,
> Then thy word doth cheer us,
> Word of consolation,
> Message of salvation.
>
> When the storms are o'er us
> And dark clouds before us,
> Then its light directeth
> And our way protecteth.
>
> Who can tell the pleasure,
> Who recount the treasure,
> By thy word imparted
> To the simple-hearted?
>
> Word of mercy, giving
> Succour to the living;
> Word of life, supplying
> Comfort to the dying.
>
> O that we, discerning
> Its most holy learning,
> Lord, may love and fear thee,
> Evermore be near thee!

Henry Williams Baker
SASB 808

11

Humility

Do nothing out of selfish ambition or vain conceit. Rather, in humility value others above yourselves, not looking to your own interests but each of you to the interests of the others. In your relationships with one another, have the same mindset as Christ Jesus.

Philippians 2:3–5

WE live in a 'me'-centred society where people strive to be better than everyone else. TV, film, magazines and social media tell us we need to be better looking, smarter and more talented than everyone else. We are also told that the only way to be a woman of worth is to be a mum, to be a man of worth is to be successful, and that we should have everything all together.

When we are trapped in this 'me'-centred mindset, we struggle to celebrate in the success of the people around us and we feel the need to compare ourselves to others, often to our own detriment. This passage turns this process completely on its head.

When we are thinking about what humility looks like, the perfect example is that of Jesus. The Son of God came with greatest humility, born in a stable. Throughout his time on Earth we saw him constantly humbling himself. His death was the greatest act of humility so that each of us might gain.

Paul tells us to have the mindset of Christ, and in the Gospel of John we are told how we can do this. He states that we must allow God to become greater and ourselves to become less. Jesus underlines this when he says:

'Love the Lord your God with all your heart and with all your soul and with all your strength and with all your mind', and 'Love your neighbour as yourself.'

Luke 10:27–28

The key to humility is love. Love for God and love for those around you. Paul in his letter to the Ephesians also makes connections between humility and love when he says: 'Be completely humble and gentle; be patient, bearing with one another in love' (Ephesians 4:2). We must love and value others and put them first in order to become humble and we must learn to love them just as Christ loves them.

Humility isn't easy. Valuing others above yourself is a sacrifice. It can cost us time, money and effort. It can mean putting your own desires on the back burner while you support others to be the person God created them to be.

In the story of Ruth, we see a woman who humbly sacrificed her life, home and religion in order to put her mother-in-law's needs first. Her humility was costly, but it was what God required of her, and it is what God requires of us too.

And what does the Lord require of you? To act justly and to love mercy and to walk humbly with your God.

Micah 6:8

When we practise humility and put others before ourselves, we are taking a risk. We risk being hurt by others if the kindness isn't reciprocated or an attitude of humility isn't shown to us. People can be insensitive and that can cause great pain. Colossians 3 explains that we do not need to practise humility in isolation, but we need a whole wardrobe of characteristics for a life in Christ to flourish.

Therefore, as God's chosen people, holy and dearly loved, clothe yourselves with compassion, kindness, humility, gentleness and patience.

Colossians 3:12

With the whole wardrobe of God in our lives, we can practise humility and become wise to any hurts that may come along. Although humility has its challenges it also has so many rewards.

> Yet he gives his grace [his undeserved favour] to the humble [those who give up self-importance].
>
> Proverbs 3:34, *AMP*

> The reward for humility and fear of the Lord is riches and honour and life.
>
> Proverbs 22:4, *NRSV*

A life of humility results in many rewards and can teach us a lot about ourselves. Living a life of humility does not mean we should see ourselves as worthless. You are fearfully and wonderfully made. You are the child of the King! What it means is that we should think of others before ourselves. We need to turn away from thinking of ourselves and look to someone else. This can be as simple as holding the door open for someone, buying them a coffee or offering to help a colleague with their workload.

On my own journey through childlessness and infertility I have found great joy in helping my sisters in Christ around me who are struggling too. I have had the absolute privilege of supporting women through the good times and the bad, and it has really taught me about humility and compassion.

When we spend our lives focused on God and his word, we start caring more about him and his love, and think less about ourselves. We are called to love others as Christ loves others – to see them through his eyes. Christ was willing to give his life for others. He made himself nothing so that we can have eternal life. Let us follow his example and look to others today.

Questions

1. How do we sometimes struggle with humility?
2. What examples of humility do we see in the Bible? How is Jesus a good example of humility?
3. Ruth's humility was costly. What may be the cost of humility in our present circumstance?
4. How does the following song relate to what we have spoken about?

Help us to help each other, Lord,
Each other's cross to bear;
Let each his friendly aid afford
And feel his brother's care.

Help us to build each other up,
Our little stock improve;
Increase our faith, confirm our hope,
And perfect us in love.

Up into thee, our living head,
Let us in all things grow,
Till thou hast made us free indeed
And spotless here below.

Charles Wesley
SASB 815

12

Prayers of Faith

At once Jesus realised that power had gone out from him. He turned round in the crowd and asked, 'Who touched my clothes?' 'You see the people crowding against you,' his disciples answered, 'and yet you can ask, "Who touched me?"' But Jesus kept looking around to see who had done it. Then the woman, knowing what had happened to her, came and fell at his feet and, trembling with fear, told him the whole truth. He said to her, 'Daughter, your faith has healed you. Go in peace and be freed from your suffering.'

Mark 5:30–34

THE woman who came to see Jesus was in a desperate way. She had been suffering with a problem for over 12 years and had reached breaking point. No matter what she did and no matter how much money she spent, she didn't get any better. In fact, she got worse! Due to her problem, she spent most of her time isolated outside the city walls. She was cut off from her friends and family, and was seen by everyone as an outcast. She felt as though she couldn't get any lower. It was only then that she sought out Jesus.

How often in life do we only come to Jesus when we are really desperate? We have exhausted all other options and it is only when we have made a mess of things in our own strength do we finally come to Jesus. When we are journeying through the wilderness of difficulties like infertility, grief or issues with our health, we often try to control all the things we can, as there is so much in our lives that we cannot control. This can stop us from coming to God as we should, and relying on his help.

The Bible is full of people who come to God in prayer. God wants us to come to him and seek him.

> If my people, who are called by my name, will humble themselves and pray and seek my face and turn from their wicked ways, then I will hear from heaven, and I will forgive their sin and will heal their land.
>
> 2 Chronicles 7:14

God is just waiting for us to come to him. When we come to him as a last resort and in desperation we miss out on such a great peace and healing. God wants us to come to him in all circumstances.

> Don't be pulled in different directions or worried about a thing. Be saturated in prayer throughout each day, offering your faith-filled requests before God with overflowing gratitude. Tell him every detail of your life, then God's wonderful peace that transcends human understanding, *will make the answers known to you* through Jesus Christ.
>
> Philippians 4:6–7, *TPT*

The woman was convinced that Jesus was the answer. She knew that with just one touch, one encounter, she would be healed. The woman came to Jesus feeling hopeless, helpless and completely forgotten, but Jesus looked at her and saw the real her, not the person that everyone else saw, and not just her problem.

Today, Jesus sees you, not as the world sees you, not even how you see yourself and not just your wilderness. But he sees you as a person of faith. Jesus asks you to come to him with the same faith the bleeding woman had.

Faith that Jesus can help us through all our problems is the key to an abundant life full of wholeness and healing. We are called to live a life by faith and not by sight. The woman in the passage had faith that God would make her whole again regardless of what the 12 years of treatment said or what she saw in front of her. God calls us to do the same in our own situation today.

> For God intended that your faith not be established on man's wisdom but by trusting in his almighty power.
>
> 1 Corinthians 2:5, *TPT*

For us today, prayer and faith go hand in hand. We must come before God, reach out, pray and believe that he will answer.

> For this reason I am telling you, whatever things you ask for in prayer [in accordance with God's will], believe [with confident trust] that you have received them, and they will be given to you.
>
> Mark 11:24, *AMP*

Questions

1. Do you ever feel that people see the things you are suffering with and not the person? How do you cope with that?
2. What strategies do you have to keep your prayer life vibrant?
3. Where in your life do you need to pray in faith? Pray some prayers of faith right now.
4. How does the following relate to what we have thought about?

What a friend we have in Jesus,
All our sins and griefs to bear!
What a privilege to carry
Everything to God in prayer!
O what peace we often forfeit,
O what needless pain we bear,
All because we do not carry
Everything to God in prayer!

Have we trials and temptations?
Is there trouble anywhere?
We should never be discouraged:
Take it to the Lord in prayer.
Can we find a friend so faithful,
Who will all our sorrows share?
Jesus knows our every weakness:
Take it to the Lord in prayer.

Are we weak and heavy laden,
Cumbered with a load of care?
Precious Saviour, still our refuge:
Take it to the Lord in prayer.
Do thy friends despise, forsake thee?
Take it to the Lord in prayer;
In his arms he'll take and shield thee,
Thou wilt find a solace there.

Joseph Medlicott Scriven
SASB 795

13

Discouragement

Cleanse me with hyssop, and I shall be clean;
wash me, and I shall be whiter than snow.
Let me hear joy and gladness;
let the bones you have crushed rejoice.
Hide your face from my sins and blot out all my iniquity.
Create in me a pure heart, O God,
and renew a steadfast spirit within me.
Do not cast me from your presence
or take your Holy Spirit from me.
Restore to me the joy of your salvation
and grant me a willing spirit, to sustain me.
Psalm 51:7–10

DAVID had messed up big time in his life! He had been a man fully sold out to God. He had reached great heights and had been used powerfully by God, but in a short space of time he felt it all crash around him. He had committed adultery and murder and had broken many of the laws God had given his people. Psalm 51 shows a broken man very aware of the things he had done. David was completely discouraged.

I'm sure that we haven't done all the things that David did, but I know we are no strangers to discouragement. The journey of childlessness and infertility can be full of despair, as can journeys of poverty, unemployment, singleness and bereavement, and this can affect our relationship with God.

Hope deferred makes the heart sick.

Proverbs 13:12, *NLT*

We, like David, can feel utterly hopeless and full of despair, but when we turn to the Psalms, especially the psalms of David, we always see that there is a thread of hope in every situation. In Psalm 51 we see that David knows his God is faithful and that he can be restored with God's help. He asks God for a pure heart and a right spirit and desires God's closeness once again. He understands that a relationship with God is more important than altars and sacrifices, but the pivitol word is *relationship*.

Sometimes our eyes can get clouded by our circumstances and despair. Sometimes our desire for a baby, or job, or husband overtakes our desire for God. But we have hope! God wants us to come close to him and share our doubt and despair with him. When we are in the pit and struggle to find hope, we are gifted with the Holy Spirit.

In the same way, the Spirit helps us in our weakness. We do not know what we ought to pray for, but the Spirit himself intercedes for us through wordless groans. And he who searches our hearts knows the mind of the Spirit, because the Spirit intercedes for God's people in accordance with the will of God.

Romans 8:26

Throughout the pages of the Bible we see stories of hope in despair. God is with each of these people even through their darkest time. God is a good God of restoration, and he promises he will be with us in every circumstance and wherever we go.

Have I not commanded you? Be strong and courageous. Do not be afraid; do not be discouraged, for the Lord your God will be with you wherever you go.

Joshua 1:9

The great news is that David's story didn't end stuck in a pit of discouragement forever. God forgave him and he continued to spread the love and faithfulness of God. In Psalm 33 we see such promise and adoration for a God who keeps his promises. David's hope was restored and his relationship with God reached a new level of closeness.

In Psalm 33 we see a prayer of hope that we can each pray today in spite of our circumstances.

> We wait in hope for the Lord;
> he is our help and our shield.
> In him our hearts rejoice,
> for we trust in his holy name.
> May your unfailing love be with us, Lord,
> even as we put our hope in you.

Psalm 33:20–22

Today we can be encouraged that God uses us in spite of our despair and our failings. Not only that, but God has fulfilled his promise through Jesus, that all our sins have been erased and we have an eternal hope.

Questions

1. How do you cope in times of discouragement and despair?
2. How can you deepen your relationship with God?
3. What is your prayer of hope today? Take some time to write one.
4. How does the following song relate to what we have thought about?

> *There is a hope that burns within my heart,*
> *That gives me strength for every passing day;*
> *A glimpse of Glory now revealed in meagre part,*

Yet drives all doubt away:
I stand in Christ, with sins forgiven;
And Christ in me, the hope of Heaven!
My highest calling and my deepest joy,
To make his will my home.

There is a hope that lifts my weary head,
A consolation strong against despair,
That when the world has plunged me in its deepest pit,
I find the Saviour there!
Through present sufferings, future's fear,
He whispers 'Courage!' in my ear.
For I am safe in everlasting arms,
And they will lead me Home.

There is a hope that stands the test of time,
That lifts my eyes beyond the beckoning grave,
To see the matchless beauty of a day divine
When I behold his face!
When sufferings cease and sorrows die,
And every longing satisfied,
Then joy unspeakable will flood my soul,
For I am truly Home.

Stuart Townend and Mark Edwards
SASB 550

14

Pour out your soul

'I am a woman who is deeply troubled. I have not been drinking wine or beer; I was pouring out my soul to the Lord. Do not take your servant for a wicked woman; I have been praying here out of my great anguish and grief.' Eli answered, 'Go in peace, and may the God of Israel grant you what you have asked of him.'

1 Samuel 1:15–17

I LOVE the story of Hannah in the Bible, and in the reading we can see a woman clinging to God's promises and trusting in his words in a time of great brokenness.

Do you ever find that some people have the ability to pick on your weak spot or provoke you concerning something you are sensitive about? It can be heartbreaking and impossible to shake. It can be as simple as people around you getting, so easily, those things which you are struggling to have. For me, a great place of sorrow and provocation can be social media. Pregnancy announcements can fill me with such grief and leave me with a feeling of hopelessness for days! These feelings are a natural part of the grief you feel. In 1 Samuel 1:6–7 we see Hannah faced a similar problem.

> Because the Lord had closed Hannah's womb, her rival kept provoking her in order to irritate her. This went on year after year. Whenever Hannah went up to the house of the Lord, her rival provoked her till she wept and would not eat.
>
> 1 Samuel 1:6–7

Hannah suffered this intense provocation for years, until one day she decided that she had had enough. She went to the place where she could find solace and assistance ... at the feet of God. She felt indescribable pain, but she understood that coming to God with her problems and laying it before him could lead to release.

Hannah in verse 15 says she is pouring out her soul to the Lord. Her prayer of faith is deep, intentional and brutally honest. Looking at Hannah's life-changing prayer, consider how often we pour out our soul to the Lord. Hannah didn't care that she looked silly, or that people thought she was drunk – she was just concerned about her business with the Lord.

The answer to her grief and sorrow was to come before God and share it all. This is something that God calls each of us to do.

> Come to me, all who are weary and burdened, and I will give you rest. Put my yoke upon your shoulders – it might appear heavy at first, but it is perfectly fitted to your curves. Learn from me, for I am gentle and humble of heart. When you are yoked to me, your weary souls will find rest. For my yoke is easy, and my burden is light.
>
> Matthew 11:28–30, *VOICE*

After Hannah had poured out her soul to God, she spent time in worship. This is a key to help each of us to grow in strength and to change the way we deal with all sorts of difficult situations. When we spend time worshipping our almighty God and reflect on his character, it helps us to put our problems into perspective and will change the way we view those things that seem to be impossible.

When Hannah had finished her time in prayer and worship, her hope in God's promises was renewed. Her encounter with God persuaded her to rely on God's promises and have absolute peace. She went home, began to eat and carried on with life. The problem hadn't gone away – I'm sure she was still often provoked – but her perspective had changed. She was singing a new song, maybe a little like this one:

But as for me, your strength shall be my song of joy. At each and every sunrise, my lyrics of your love will fill the air! For you have been my glory-fortress, a stronghold in my day of distress. O my strength, I sing with joy your praises. O my stronghold, I sing with joy your song! O my Saviour, I sing with joy the lyrics of your faithful love for me!

Psalm 59:16–17, TPT

God blessed Hannah and gave her a son, but through this I think the greater promise that was fulfilled was the completeness that only God can bring and the peace that comes from a soul poured out and laid before God. Later in that story, her complete trust in God enabled her to give up her precious son for the work he had in store for him.

God wants us to come before him and pour out our soul. That is why he sent Jesus down to Earth, so we can be in relationship with him. Because of Jesus' sacrifice, we can freely come before his throne and leave with a brand new perspective.

Questions

1. What things provoke you and threaten to fill you with a sense of hopelessness?

2. When did you last pour out your soul to the Lord? Why do you think that it is important?

3. What worship songs help you to shift your perspective? Make a playlist of helpful songs.

4. How does the following song relate to what we have thought about?

When I'm tired and nothing's going right for me;
When things I've counted on just do not come my way;
When in my mind the thick grey folds of doubt arise,
It's then I seem to hear him say:

Chorus
Share my yoke and find that I am joined with you,
Your slightest movement I shall feel and be there too!
Share my yoke and come the way that I must go!
In our 'togetherness' my peace you'll know;
The word beholding us will see it so!

When I'm perplexed and no one's understanding me;
When even safest thoughts collapse in disarray;
When I've lost the things that always seemed so sure,
It's then I need to hear him say:

When I'm alone and nothing's getting through to me;
An isolation that increases day by day;
When closest friends can seem a thousand miles away,
It's then I long to hear him say:

Joy Webb
SASB 527

15

Trust through devastation

Then he sent out a dove to see if the water had receded from the surface of the ground. But the dove could find nowhere to perch because there was water over all the surface of the earth; so it returned to Noah in the ark. He reached out his hand and took the dove and brought it back to himself in the ark. He waited seven more days and again sent out the dove from the ark. When the dove returned to him in the evening, there in its beak was a freshly plucked olive leaf! Then Noah knew that the water had receded from the earth.

Genesis 8:8–11

IN THE story of Noah and the ark, we see that he had a really dramatic time. He followed the Lord closely and had been assigned a pretty big task to do. It must have seemed like an almost impossible task for an almost unthinkable reason. However, Noah trusted in God despite the seeming impossibility, and went ahead with building the boat.

Noah's faith held him through a time of 'impossibility'. The people around him must have thought he was mad to build an ark in the middle of the land. I'm sure people laughed at him. He must have felt very isolated watching others live life while he was stuck trying to achieve the impossible. Does this sound familiar to you? Often in the pursuit of gaining what we really desire, we can feel isolated, as though we are trying to achieve the impossible, while others seem to continue through their life with ease.

Noah had faith that the impossible was possible and we see that the God of the impossible is on every page of the Bible.

> God can do anything, you know – far more than you could ever imagine or guess or request in your wildest dreams!
>
> Ephesians 3:20, *MSG*

When we see pictures on the TV of flooding or even experience it first hand, it is absolutely devastating. It is awful to imagine seeing everything you once possessed being so completely destroyed. It must have been overwhelming for Noah and his family to see the whole earth destroyed. It really must have seemed like the end of the world.

Noah was certain God would remember him despite what the world around him looked like. He trusted that God's promises would be fulfilled – he sent out birds regularly in the hope that the news would be good. Even when it first seemed hopeless, he trusted in God and was patient in waiting.

On our bad days it can feel to us like our world is ending! We can look at our life and it looks so different from what we once expected it to be. We must be encouraged to trust in God with hope and patience.

> May the God of hope fill you with all joy and peace as you trust in him, so that you may overflow with hope by the power of the Holy Spirit.
>
> Romans 15:15

God never forgot Noah and he rewarded his faith by making a great covenant with him and his descendants (that includes us!). He also gave the symbol of a rainbow to remind his people of his great love. The Bible is full of promises for us too. Promises that we must hold on to in the bad times and the good. Promises like:

> I have told you these things, so that in me you may have peace. In the world you will have trouble. But take heart! I have overcome the world.
>
> John 16:33

He gives power to the weak
   and strength to the powerless.
Even youths will become weak and tired,
   and young men will fall in exhaustion.
But those who trust in the Lord will find new strength.
   They will soar high on wings like eagles.
They will run and not grow weary.
   They will walk and not faint.

Isaiah 40:29–31, NLT

Does your life seem like a big flood? Do you sometimes feel as if all around you is devastation? Hold tight! Be patient in your waiting and cling to the promises he has made to you. God will fulfil his promises and he will send you a rainbow.

Questions

1. How have you felt isolated when trying to fulfil God's calling? How did you stay committed to the task?

2. How can we be more patient in our waiting and trusting?

3. What promises has God given you from Scripture? How have they helped you? Speak some promises of Scripture over yourself and others.

4. How does the following song relate to what we have thought about?

Standing on the promises of Christ my King,
Through eternal ages let his praises ring;
Glory in the highest, I will shout and sing,
Standing on the promises of God.

Chorus
Standing, standing,
Standing on the promises of God my Saviour;

Standing, standing,
I'm standing on the promises of God.

Standing on the promises that cannot fail,
When the howling winds of doubt and fear assail;
By the living word of God I shall prevail,
Standing on the promises of God.

Standing on the promises of Christ my Lord,
Bound to him eternally by love's strong cord,
Overcoming daily with the Spirit's sword,
Standing on the promises of God.

Standing on the promises I cannot fall,
Listening every moment to the Spirit's call,
Resting in my Saviour as my all in all,
Standing on the promises of God.

Standing on the promises I now can see,
Perfect, present cleansing in the blood for me;
Standing in the liberty where Christ makes free,
Standing on the promises of God.

Russell Kelso Carter
SASB 522

16.

Love yourself

'"Love the Lord your God with all your heart, and with all your soul and with all your mind and with all your strength." The second [commandment] is this: "Love your neighbour as yourself." There is no commandment greater than these.'
Mark 12:30–31

OFTEN when we think about loving our neighbour as ourselves we think about how we may love our neighbour and who our neighbour might be. But what about loving yourself? How can we love others when we struggle to love ourselves?

We have all faced rejection – be it from family, friends, colleagues, work, relationships or even church. We allow how others see us to dictate how we see ourselves, rather than clinging to what the word says we are. Sometimes we can struggle to see ourselves as God sees us.

Walking difficult roads like that of childlessness, singleness and grief, we often struggle with the idea of loving ourselves. It can be so difficult to love ourselves when our body doesn't seem to be working right. We feel as if we are simply not good enough.

But let me tell you today – *you are good enough.* You are the apple of God's eye just as you are. You are loved in a beautiful way.

> The Lord your God is with you,
> the Mighty Warrior who saves.
> He will take great delight in you;

in his love he will no longer rebuke you,
but will rejoice over you with singing.

Zephaniah 3:17

There will always be people who will tell us that we are not good enough. The media bombard us with images of the perfect body, the perfect clothes and the perfect personality. The media tell us that we can only ever be perfect if we are married with 2.4 children. This can make our battle to love ourselves even harder.

However, when you start to feel unlovable, look to the word of God. The word says there is nothing you can do that will ever make God love you any more or any less. You are so loved by him.

Who shall separate us from the love of Christ? Shall trouble or hardship or persecution or famine or nakedness or danger or sword? As it is written:

'For your sake we face death all day long; we are considered as sheep to be slaughtered.'

No, in all these things we are more than conquerors through him who loved us. For I am convinced that neither death nor life, neither angels nor demons, neither the present nor the future, nor any powers, neither height nor depth, nor anything else in all creation, will be able to separate us from the love of God that is in Christ Jesus our Lord.

Romans 8:35–39

Nothing can separate us from God's love – nothing that we are facing, not infertility or childlessness or singleness.

So, beautiful child of God, love yourself! You are loved by the King of kings and the Creator of the universe! You are loved so much by God that he sent his Son to die for you so that you can live in freedom.

Knowing that you are loved by God will change the way you see yourself and will give you boldness to serve those around you. In Luke 7:36–50 we see a beautiful story about a woman who anointed Jesus' feet with perfume and her own tears. She stepped out tenaciously and showed her love for him even though others didn't understand. Jesus rewarded her and it changed her life completely.

'Therefore, I tell you, her many sins have been forgiven – as her great love has shown.'

Luke 7:47

When you too grab hold of this truth of God, it will completely transform the way you view yourself and others. When you know you are loved by God, you can love yourself and love others as well. When you know you are loved by God, you can respect yourself and others. When you know you are loved by God, you can care about yourself and show care for others.

Questions

1. Do you struggle to love yourself? In what ways can you learn to love yourself better?
2. How does society and the media affect the way you love yourself? What Bible verses can you use to combat this?
3. Looking at the story of the woman who anointed Jesus, how does the realisation of God's love for you help you to love others?
4. How does the following song relate to what we have thought about?

Loved with everlasting love,
Led by grace that love to know;
Spirit, breathing from above,
Thou has taught me this is so.
O this full and perfect peace!
O this transport all divine!
In a love which cannot cease
I am his and he is mine.

Heaven above is softer blue,
Earth around is sweeter green;
Something lives in every hue,
Christless eyes have never seen;
Birds with gladder songs o'erflow,
Flowers with deeper beauties shine,
Since I know, as now I know,
I am his and he is mine.

His for ever, only his;
Who the Lord and me shall part?
Ah! with what a rest of bliss
Christ can fill the loving heart.
Heaven and earth may fade and flee,
First-born light in gloom decline,
But, throughout eternity,
I am his and he is mine.

George Wade Robinson
SASB 723

17

Trust and obey

'Which of you, if your son asks for bread, will give him a stone? Or if he asks for a fish, will give him a snake? If you, then, though you are evil, know how to give good gifts to your children, how much more will your Father in heaven give good gifts to those who ask him! So in everything, do to others what you would have them do to you, for this sums up the Law and the Prophets.'

Matthew 7:9–12

I HAVE two beautiful dogs, and one of the challenges of being a dog owner is disciplining your pet. Initially when one of them misbehaves, I will warn them to stop their bad behaviour. If the bad behaviour continues, there will be a consequence to their actions.

After a few times of disciplining them, they will inevitably learn to be good!

This is often what it is like with God. He will show us the right way and it is up to us whether we follow him or not. God knows what is best for us. As our heavenly Father, he can see the bigger picture and wants us to succeed.

> Yet you, O Lord, are our Father. We are the clay, you are the potter; we are all the work of your hand.
>
> Isaiah 64:8

God talks a lot about us being his children as it is a great illustration of surrender and obedience.

Throughout the pages of the Old Testament we see the story of Father God and his children – the people of Israel. We see often that God knows what is best for the people of Israel, but they disobey and fail to trust in him. There is always a consequence to their disobedience, including them spending 40 years on a journey that could have taken them a matter of days!

> The Israelites had moved about in the wilderness forty years until all the men who were of military age when they left Egypt had died, since they had not obeyed the Lord. For the Lord had sworn to them that they would not see the land he had solemnly promised their ancestors to give us, a land flowing with milk and honey.
>
> Joshua 5:6

We must trust in the fact that God, as our Father, knows what is best and wants us to be happy. We may think that we know what will make us happy or content, but true contentment comes only by trusting in him and being obedient to his word.

Today you may feel like the children of Israel wandering around the desert. You may feel as if your heavenly Father has given you a snake instead of a fish or a stone instead of bread. But be assured, God wants what is best for you and is asking you to turn to him in obedience.

> And this is love: that we walk in obedience to his commands. As you have heard from the beginning, his command is that you walk in love.
>
> 2 John 1:6

There is a great hymn at the end of this chapter that says it all when it comes to surrender. It was written by a man who was moved by a young man's testimony and declaration: 'I'm not quite sure, but I'm going to trust and I'm going to obey.'

The second verse of this song is particularly true for us as we walk through difficult times. What we are facing is not a punishment from God in any way, but when we surrender and give our sorrows and burdens to him, he will repay us for our grief and richly bless us.

Questions

1. Do you really believe that God wants what is best for you? What Scriptures do you know that tell you God is for you?

2. Have you ever had a period of time in disobedience like the children of Israel? How did you shift your focus to God?

3. How is walking in obedience to God's command a sign of love? How can we do this better?

4. How does the following song relate to what we have thought about?

When we walk with the Lord
In the light of his word,
What a glory he sheds on our way;
While we do his good will,
He abides with us still
And with all who will trust and obey.

Chorus
Trust and obey, for there's no other way
To be happy in Jesus,
but to trust and obey.

Not a burden we bear,
Not a sorrow we share,
But our toil he doth richly repay;
Not a grief nor a loss,
Not a frown nor a cross,
But is blessed if we trust and obey.

Then in fellowship sweet
We will sit at his feet,
Or we'll walk by his side in the way;
What he says we will do,
Where he sends we will go,
Never fear, only trust and obey.

John Henry Sammis
SASB 690

18

Waiting

**Trust in the Lord with all your heart and lean not on your
own understanding; in all your ways submit to him, and he
will make your paths straight.**

Proverbs 3:5–6

GOD'S word promises us that he will give us great things if we
live a life completely committed to him … But he doesn't say
when! When it comes to waiting, sometimes it can be extremely
hard to fix our eyes on him and not rely on what we can see in
the situation.

I remember when all of my friends started to find long-term
relationships and get married. It was a really difficult time for me.
The desire of my heart was to be a wife and mother, but I couldn't
see how God was going to do it. I blamed myself for the long wait
… I thought I wasn't good enough, pretty enough, funny enough,
or simply not marriage material.

However, after a while I came to the realisation – a God-given
realisation. God asked me what I was focusing on; was it my
desires, or God? You see, we have to be focused on the right things.
We must choose to fix our eyes on Jesus and focus on the things
that God instructs to focus on in his word.

You will keep in perfect peace those whose minds are steadfast,
because they trust in you.

Isaiah 26:3

It is only through focusing on him through the waiting that we receive the things we desire and understand that they come from him. God gives us instructions on what to do in those days when things are tough and we start to doubt who we are in him.

> Finally, brothers and sisters, whatever is true, whatever is noble, whatever is right, whatever is pure, whatever is lovely, whatever is admirable – if anything is excellent or praiseworthy – think about such things.
>
> Philippians 4:8

The Passion Translation of the key verses says:

> Trust in the Lord completely, and do not rely on your own opinions. With all your heart rely on him to guide you, and he will lead you in every decision you make. Become intimate with him in whatever you do, and he will lead you wherever you go. Don't think for a moment that you know it all, for wisdom comes when you adore him with undivided devotion and avoid everything that's wrong.
>
> Proverbs 3:5–7, *TPT*

I love the phrase that says: 'Don't think for a moment that you know it all.' We live in a society that tells us that we should know it all, demand it all and never wait for anything. However, the Bible often tells us to live a counter-cultural life, and this is no exception. The verse tell us that our wisdom comes from God and that we must trust in him through all our times of waiting, even if it seems a lonely road.

Today you need to know that you are not alone!

In the Bible we see so many stories of people who lived a life sold out for God and wanted to receive the things they desired. Sarah waited for a child, Joseph waited to be released from prison, Moses waited for his mission to become clear, Ruth waited to be happy again, Hannah waited for her promised child, and the list goes on and on!

God gave me my desired husband after a long wait (and he was so worth the wait!) but God used that time to prepare me and help me to be the best wife I can be. I was also given the opportunity to minister to people as a single woman in a way I cannot as a married woman. I am still waiting to be a mother and now I see the friends who found love when I was single having babies. This is tough and some days it seems so impossible. It can be so easy to slip back into thinking I am not good enough, or have enough favour with God.

But when I look to the word and the long list of people who also had to wait for the desires of their heart, I see who I am in Christ. I may try to go my own way and rely on my own ideas, but I will inevitably find God's way is best. *The Voice* translation of Proverbs 3:5–6 says: 'Place your trust in the Eternal; rely on him completely; never depend upon your own ideas and inventions. Give him the credit for everything you accomplish, and he will smooth out and straighten the road that lies ahead.'

Questions

1. What strategies do you have to fix your eyes on God through the times of waiting?

2. Which Bible characters and their waits inspire you when you are in a time of waiting?

3. What true, noble, right, pure, lovely and admirable things do you think of when you doubt yourself and in your waiting?

4. How does the following song relate to what we have thought about?

> *When I ponder o'er the story*
> *Of my life's defeat and grief,*
> *How much misery and blindness*
> *I can trace to unbelief!*
> *O how many fights I've lost,*
> *All for want of faith to trust!*

Chorus
O for a deeper, O for a greater,
O for a perfect trust in the Lord!

Can I wonder I have faltered?
Can I be surprised to fall?
When my faith could most have saved me,
I have trusted least of all.
When my own resources fail,
Then his power should most prevail.

If to grace there is no limit,
Why should I be slow to plead?
If thy power is not restricted,
Why not speak my every need?
All the treasures of his throne,
Faith will make them all my own.

Yes, dear Saviour, I will trust thee,
Live by faith and not by sight,
Knowing thou art close beside me,
Giving victory in the fight.
Jesus, while thou art so near,
I will never, never fear.

Cornelie Ida Ernestine Booth
SASB 740

19

Seasons

There is a time for everything, and a season for every activity under the heavens.

Ecclesiastes 3:1

I LOVE watching the seasons of nature come and go throughout the year. Some seasons seem really fruitful, full of pretty flowers and birds and everything seems to be in abundance. While other seasons, although still beautiful, seem bare and somewhat empty.

The Bible talks a lot about seasons, both natural and spiritual. There is a time for every season in our life; every season has a purpose, maybe to grow, maybe to store, maybe to blossom and maybe to show great beauty. We can learn so much about nature and ecology through the seasons of nature and the same is true in our own life. We learn new things in new seasons.

As we walk through the wilderness of our circumstances, we have a lot to learn. Our desire may be for a different season, but we can learn so much about God, ourselves and our relationships. We have, in our current season, more time for God, a chance to go deeper in him and a chance to build and grow solid relationships with other brothers and sisters in Christ.

When we spend our season immersed in his word, he will do mighty things:

As the rain and the snow come down from heaven, and do not return to it without watering the earth and making it bud and flourish, so that it yields seeds for the sower and bread for the eater, so is my word that goes out from my mouth: it will not return to me empty, but will accomplish what I desire and achieve the purpose for which I sent it.

Isaiah 55:10–11

In every season we find ourselves in, we should strive not only to learn from it but to truly embrace it. In some of the seasons that appear quite barren in nature, there is actually a lot going on below the ground and inside the plants. The same is true in our season of apparent barrenness. God can and will do great things in this season if we just embrace it. *The Passion Translation* puts it in a lovely way:

And don't allow yourselves to be weary or disheartened in planting good seeds, for the season of reaping the wonderful harvest you've planted is coming! Take advantage of every opportunity to be a blessing to others, especially to our brothers and sisters in the family of faith!

Galatians 6:9, *TPT*

Sometimes we can really struggle through our season. It may be difficult to embrace the season when we feel 'snowed in' and both the days and nights seem so dark. However, God promises to be with us in the dark: 'So do not fear, for I am with you; do not be dismayed, for I am your God. I will strengthen you and help you; I will uphold you with my righteous right hand' (Isaiah 41:10).

When we are content in our season, content being sold out for God right where we are, amazing things will happen.

Every season will come to an end and a new one will begin. Your seasons of emptiness will give way to blooms. When this happens, God will sing this song over you:

See! The winter is past; the rains are over and gone. Flowers appear on the earth; the season of singing has come, the cooing of doves is heard in our land. The fig-tree forms its early fruit; the blossoming vines spread their fragrance. Arise, come, my darling; my beautiful one, come with me.

Song of Songs 2:11–13

Questions

1. Name something that you have learnt in your current season.
2. How have you tried to embrace the season that you are currently in? Has it always been easy?
3. What can you do to remind yourself of God's presence when you feel snowed in?
4. How does the following song relate to what we have thought about?

God who touchest earth with beauty,
Make my heart anew;
With thy Spirit recreate me
Pure and strong and true.
Like thy springs and running waters,
Make me crystal pure;
Like thy rocks of towering grandeur,
Make me strong and sure.

Like thy dancing waves in sunlight,
Make me glad and free;
Like the straightness of the pine trees
Let me upright be.
Like the arching of the heavens,
Lift my thoughts above;
Turn my dreams to noble action,
Ministries of love.

Like the birds that soar while singing,
Give my heart a song;
May the music of thanksgiving
Echo clear and strong.
God who touches earth with beauty,

SEASONS

Make my heart anew;
Keep me ever by thy Spirit
Pure and strong and true.

Mary Susanne Edgar
SASB 320